First World War
and Army of Occupation
War Diary
France, Belgium and Germany

57 DIVISION
171 Infantry Brigade
Headquarters
1 September 1915 - 29 February 1916

WO95/2980/1

The Naval & Military Press Ltd
www.nmarchive.com
Published in association with The National Archives

Published by

The Naval & Military Press Ltd

Unit 10 Ridgewood Industrial Park,

Uckfield, East Sussex,

TN22 5QE England

Tel: +44 (0) 1825 749494

www.naval-military-press.com

www.nmarchive.com

This diary has been reprinted in facsimile from the original. Any imperfections are inevitably reproduced and the quality may fall short of modern type and cartographic standards.

© **Crown Copyright**
Images reproduced by permission of The National Archives, London, England, 2015.

Contents

Document type	Place/Title	Date From	Date To
Heading	WO95/2980-1		
Heading	57th Division 171st Infy Bde Brigade Headquarters 1915 Sep-1916 Feb And 1917 Feb-1917 Dec		
Heading	Hqrs. 171st Infy. Bde War Diary Sept 1915		
War Diary	Canterbury	01/09/1915	30/09/1915
Miscellaneous	171st Infantry Brigade	01/09/1915	01/09/1915
Heading	Head Qrs 171st Infantry Bde War Diary October 1915		
War Diary	Canterbury	01/10/1915	31/10/1915
Heading	War Diary Headquarters 171st Infy Bde November 1915		
War Diary	Canterbury	01/11/1915	30/11/1915
Heading	War Diary Dec 1st-31st 1915 Head Qrs 171st Infy Bde		
War Diary	Canterbury	01/12/1915	31/01/1916
Heading	Headquarters, 171st Infantry Brigade War Diary (Special) Feb 20th-Feb 29th 1916		
War Diary	Canterbury	01/02/1916	29/02/1916

WD 957/2480 (1)

WD 957/2980 (1)

57TH DIVISION
171ST INFY. BDE

BRIGADE HEADQUARTERS

~~FEB - DEC 1917~~

1915 SEP - 1916 FEB
AND
1917 FEB - 1917 DEC

Confidential

Hqrs. 171st Infy. Bde

War Diary

Sept 1915

Army Form C. 2118.

WAR DIARY
or
INTELLIGENCE SUMMARY.
(Erase heading not required.)

Instructions regarding War Diaries and Intelligence Summaries are contained in F. S. Regs., Part II. and the Staff Manual respectively. Title pages will be prepared in manuscript.

Place	Date	Hour	Summary of Events and Information	Remarks and references to Appendices
	1915.			
CANTERBURY.	Sept.1.		Nothing to report.	
	2.		Field Operations.	
	3.		2nd N.C.Os. Class concluded.	
	4.		3rd N.C.Os. Class commenced under Sergt.Brumhill. 2/Lt.N.B.Ronald, 1/6th K.L.R., reported at Brigade Headquarters for instructional purposes.	
	8.		Brigadier-General A.R.Gilbert D.S.O. re-assumed command of Brigade on return G.O.C., 57th (West Lancs.) Division. 2/7th and 2/8th Bns: K.L.R., removed from Hutments at Old Park into billets in Canterbury in order to make room for Divl: R.A., concentrated at Canterbury. Staff Captain inspected all Billets.	
	9.		G.O.C., proceeded round Coast with G.O.C. 57th (W.L.) Div: and General Martin.	
	10.		G.O.C. inspected training.	
	11.		" " "	
	12.		" " "	
	13.		" " "	
	14.		" " "	
	15.		Field operations. 2/7th K.L.R., bivouaced during the night at Waltham.	
	16.		G.O.C.171st Infantry Brigade assumed command of 57th Division,and Lt.Col.G.Rippon, 2/5th K.L.R. of 171st Brigade.	

Army Form C. 2118.

WAR DIARY
or
INTELLIGENCE SUMMARY.
(Erase heading not required.)

Instructions regarding War Diaries and Intelligence Summaries are contained in F.S. Regs., Part II. and the Staff Manual respectively. Title pages will be prepared in manuscript.

Place	Date	Hour	Summary of Events and Information	Remarks and references to Appendices
	Sept. 17.		Usual Routine.	
		20.	5000 sandbags despatched to Margate.	
		21.	Br.Genl.A.R.Gilbert D.S.O. re-assumed command of 171st Infantry Brigade on return of G.O.C. 57th (W.L.) Division - 3000 sandbags despatched to Herne Bay.	
		22.	4th class for junior N.C.Os. commenced under Sergt. Brumhill.	
		23.	Field Operation is neighbourhood of Petham	
		30.	Major.H.A.Fulton, Brigade Major, 171st Infantry Brigade, left for service overseas.	

E.P.Dixon.
.... Bd. General.
Comdg. 171st. Infantry Brigade.

UNIT BRIGADE.   171st Infantry Brigade.

DIVISION.   57th (West Lancashire) Division.

MOBILIZATION CENTRE.   Liverpool.

TEMPORARY WAR STATION.   Canterbury.

STATIONS OCCUPIED SINCE   Liverpool (Mersey Coast Defences)
MOBILIZATION.
                                 Knowsley.

                                 London - Guarding L.S.W. Railway and
                                          L.B.& S.C. Railway.

                                 Sevenoaks.   Canterbury.

(a) Mobilization.   The Brigade originally mobilized at
                                 Liverpool.

(b) Concentration.   2/5th Liverpool Regt - Canterbury in
                                                           billets.
                                 2/7th   ,,   ,,   Canterbury in
                                                           hutments.
                                 2/8th   ,,   ,,   Canterbury in
                                                           hutments.
                                 2/6th   ,,   ,,   Upstreet under
                                                           canvass.

(c) Organisation for   Two Battalions at Old Park.
    defence.   One Battalion at Canterbury.
                                 One Battalion at Upstreet.

(d) Training.   Battalion and Company Training carried
                                 out. Musketry proceeded with at
                                 Sandwich.   Night work practiced twice
                                 per week.   Brigade Field Operations
                                 weekly.

(e) Discipline.   Satisfactory.

(f) Administration.   (1) Medical Services - Satisfactory.
                                 (2) Veterinary   ,,   Satisfactory.
                                 (3) Supply   ,,   Satisfactory.
                                 (4) Transport   ,,   The civilian
                                     carts & harness issued at mobiliz-
                                     ation are still in use.   Indents
                                     to replace wornout harness have
                                     been submitted.
                                 (5) Ordnance Services.
                                 (6) Billeting & Hutting. Two Battalions
                                     are in Hutments, which are quite
                                     satisfactory. One Battalion is in
                                     billets, and one under canvass -
                                     both quite satisfactory.

                                 (7) Channels of correspondence in
                                     Routine matters. 57th (West Lancs)
                                     Division.

                                 (8) Range Construction. Nil, since last
                                     report.

                                 (9) Supply of Remounts. 8 Riding cobs
                                     received since last report.

(g) Reorganisation of　　　　Nil, since last Report.
　　T.F.Units:
　　Home & Imperial
　　Services.

(h) Preparation of Units　　　Nil, since last Report.
　　for Imperial
　　Service.

　　　　　　　　　　　　　　　　　　E. Pepper.
　　　　　　　　　　　　　　　　　　　Lieut-Colonel,
　　　　　　　　　　　　　Commanding 171st Infantry Brigade.

Canterbury,
　　1st September, 1915.

~~Confidential~~

Head Qrs
171st Infantry Bde

War Diary
October 1915

Army Form C. 2118.

171st INFANTRY BRIGADE.

WAR DIARY
or
INTELLIGENCE SUMMARY.

(Erase heading not required.)

Place	Date	Hour	Summary of Events and Information	Remarks and references to Appendices
Canterbury.	1915. Oct. 1.		Lt.Col S.S.G.Cohen assumed command of 2/5th K.L.R., vice Lt.Col.G.Rippon transferred to 2/8th K.L.R.	
	2		G.O.G. inspected training.	
	3		Major H.R.Sandilands, Northumberland Fusiliers, reported as Brigade Major, vice Major H.A. Fulton, proceeded Overseas.	
	4		G.O.C. inspected training.	
	5		" " " "	
	6		Lecture by Brigade Major to 2/7th and 2/8th Battalions at Old Park.	
	7		5th Class for N.C.Os under Sergt. Brumhill started.	
	8		2/8th K.L.R. returned into Hutments at Old Park.	
	9		2/7th K.L.R. returned to Hutments, Old Park.	
	10		G.O.C. inspected Training.	
	11		" " " "	
	12		Lecture by Brigade Major to 2/5th K.L.R.	
	13		2/5th, 2/7th and 2/8th K.L.R. paraded at Old Park at 2 p.m. for inspection by Munitions Representative.	
	14		2/6th K.L.R. paraded 10 a.m. at Upstreet for inspection by Munitions Representative.	
	15		G.O.C inspected Training.	
	16		" " " "	
	17		" " " "	
	18		" " " "	
	19		" " " "	
	20		2/6th K.L.R. moved from Upstreet Camp into Billets, Canterbury.	
	21		G.O.C. inspected Training.	
	22		" " " "	
	23		" " " "	
	24		" " " "	
	25		" " " "	
	26		6th Class for N.C.Os under Sergt. Brumhill started.	
	27		2nd Lieut. N.B.Ronald rejoined 2/6th K.L.R. after instruction in Brigade Staff work.	

Army Form C. 2118.

WAR DIARY
or
INTELLIGENCE SUMMARY.
(Erase heading not required.)

Place	Date	Hour	Summary of Events and Information	Remarks and references to Appendices
Canterbury	Oct. 28.		Capt. L.M.Holland, 2/6th K.L.R., attached to Brigade Headquarters for instruction. 2nd Lieut. G.L.Taylor, 2/5th K.L.R., appointed Brigade Machine Gun Officer, and joined Brigade Headquarters.	
	29.		Brigade Field Operations near Whitstable.	
	30.		,, ,, ,, ,,	
	31.		G.O.C. inspected Training.	

Castleden Lodge,
CANTERBURY.

November, 1915.

[signature] Brigadier-General,
Commanding 171st Infantry Brigade.

Confidential

War Diary

Head Quarters
171st Infy: Bde

November 1915

Canterbury
4.12.1915

Army Form C. 2118.

171st INFANTRY BRIGADE.

WAR DIARY
or
INTELLIGENCE SUMMARY.

(Erase heading not required.)

Instructions regarding War Diaries and Intelligence Summaries are contained in F.S. Regs., Part II. and the Staff Manual respectively. Title pages will be prepared in manuscript.

Place	Date	Hour	Summary of Events and Information	Remarks and references to Appendices
Canterbury.	1915. Nov.	1	G.O.C. inspected training.	
		2	" " "	
		3	" " "	
		4	Field Operations near WHITSTABLE - 2/5th and 2/6th Battalions.	
		5	" " " - 2/7th and 2/8th Battalions.	
		6	Lecture by Brigade Major on Horsemastership.	
		7	G.O.C. inspected training.	
		8	Special Observation Parties sent to Sturry, Barham and Wootton.	
		9	G.O.C. inspected training.	
		10	" " "	
		11	Field Operations in neighbourhood of BRIDGE.	
		12	Lecture on Horsemastership by Brigade Major.	
		13	G.O.C. inspected training.	
		14	" " "	
		15	G.O.C. inspected training.	
		16	Brigade Reserve .256 Ammunition handed over by 2/1st R.F.A.,	
		17	G.O.C. inspected training.	
		18	Transport inspection by General Landon.	
		19	Lecture by Brigade Major on Horsemastership.	
		20	G.O.C. inspected training.	
		21	Arrival of 525 .303 Rifles per Battalion.	
		22	Jap. Rifles despatched, with ammunition, to Weedon.	
		23	G.O.C. inspected 2/7th and 2/8th Battalions at Old Park.	
		24	" " 2/5th Battalion.	
		25	2/7th and 2/8th Battalions inspected by General Dickson.	
		26	2/5th and 2/6th " " " "	
			Lecture by Brigade Major on Musketry.	
			75 men per Battalion detailed for duty on Coast with 2/1st Kent Cyclists.	
		27	G.O.C. inspected training.	

Army Form C. 2118.

WAR DIARY
or
INTELLIGENCE SUMMARY.
(Erase heading not required.)

Instructions regarding War Diaries and Intelligence Summaries are contained in F. S. Regs., Part II. and the Staff Manual respectively. Title pages will be prepared in manuscript.

Place	Date	Hour	Summary of Events and Information	Remarks and references to Appendices
			2.	
Canterbury	Nov.	28	G.O.C. inspected training.	
		29	,, ,,	
		30	,, ,,	

CANTERBURY.

5th December, 1915.

A. Allen Brigadier-General,
Commanding 171st Infantry Brigade.

1577 Wt.W10791/1773 500,000 1/15 D. D. & L.   A.D.S.S./Forms/C. 2118.

Confidential

War Diary

Dec 1st — 31st 1915

HeadQrs 171st Infy Bde.

Army Form C. 2118.

WAR DIARY
or
INTELLIGENCE SUMMARY
(Erase heading not required.)

Instructions regarding War Diaries and Intelligence Summaries are contained in F. S. Regs., Part II. and the Staff Manual respectively. Title pages will be prepared in manuscript.

Hour, Date, Place	Summary of Events and Information	Remarks and references to Appendices
Canterbury Dec 1st 1915	GOC inspects training	WD
2nd	2nd/Lt St. Hughes 2/5th KLR reports for duty with Bde H.Qrs	WD
3rd	GOC inspects training - Lecture by Bde Major on Horse Mastership - Inspection on Mess Parade by OC No 3 Co ASC of Bde 1st Army Transport	WD
4th		WD
5th		WD
6th		WD
7th	GOC inspects trains. "	WD
	Parties of 217. 218. KLR proceed to RYE for modern gun Course - under B.M.G.O.	WD
8th	87 other Ranks 2/8th KLR transferred to Pont. Bn. C. of letter 10697 A-5/10.9.15.	WD
10th	GOC Brigade reports at HQrs 2nd Army - Field operations at BARHAM	WD
13th	Lecture by Bde Major.	WD

127. W 3299 200,000 (E) 8/14 J.B.C. & A. Forms/C. 2118/11.

Army Form C. 2118.

WAR DIARY
or
INTELLIGENCE SUMMARY
(Erase heading not required.)

Instructions regarding War Diaries and Intelligence Summaries are contained in F. S. Regs., Part II. and the Staff Manual respectively. Title pages will be prepared in manuscript.

Hour, Date, Place	Summary of Events and Information	Remarks and references to Appendices
Cinderton Lee 1915 14	Genl inspection training	M.S.
15	"	M.S.
16	"	M.S.
17	Lecture by Bde Major on Musketry	M.S.
18		M.S.
19	Lecture by Bde Major Horse Masters'hip	M.S.
20	Inspection of 2/5 2/7 KLR by GOC 2nd Army	M.S.
28	Parties of 2/5 & 2/6 KLR proceeded to SANDWICH for machine gun Course instr. B.A.G.O.	M.S.
29		

M Lundwig Major
for Bde Major
Bt. General
Comdg. 171st Infantry Brigade.

Army Form C. 2118.

HQ 171 BDE

WAR DIARY
or
INTELLIGENCE SUMMARY.
(Erase heading not required.)

Instructions regarding War Diaries and Intelligence Summaries are contained in F.S. Regs., Part II and the Staff Manual respectively. Title pages will be prepared in manuscript.

Place	Date 1916	Hour	Summary of Events and Information	Remarks and references to Appendices
CANTERBURY	Jan 1		Nil	nil
	" 2		Nil	nil
	" 3	9 a.m.	B⁺ General A.R. GILBERT D.S.O. proceeds to FRANCE on tour of instruction. Lt Col G. RIPPON assumes temporary command.	nil
	" 4	11 a.m.	Lt General WOOLCOMBE C.B. Comdg 2ᵈ Army inspects 2/6ᵗʰ & 2/8ᵗʰ K.L.R. in Bayonet fighting, Musketry, Drill and Physical Training.	nil
	" 5		Nil	nil
	" 6		Nil	nil
	" 7	5 p.m.	B⁺ General A.R. GILBERT D.S.O. resumes command	nil
	" 8		Nil	nil
	" 9		Nil	nil
	" 10		Nil	nil
	" 11		Nil	nil
	" 12		Nil	nil
	" 13		Nil	nil
	" 14		Nil	nil
	" 15		Nil	nil
	" 16		Nil	nil
	" 17		Nil	nil
	" 18		Nil	nil

Army Form C. 2118.

WAR DIARY
or
INTELLIGENCE SUMMARY.

(Erase heading not required.)

Instructions regarding War Diaries and Intelligence Summaries are contained in F. S. Regs., Part II. and the Staff Manual respectively. Title pages will be prepared in manuscript.

Place	Date 1916	Hour	Summary of Events and Information	Remarks and references to Appendices
CANTERBURY	Jan. 19		Nil	
"	" 20		Nil	
"	" 21		Nil	
"	" 22		Nil	
"	" 23		Nil	
"	" 24	3 p.m.	Practice Fire Alarm	
"	" 25		Nil	
"	" 26		Nil	
"	" 27		Nil	
"	" 28		Nil	
"	" 29		Nil	
"	" 30		Nil	
"	" 31		Between Jan. 22nd and 31st recruits called up from Derby Groups have joined as under:— 2/5th K.L.R. 92 2/6th K.L.R. 133 2/7th K.L.R. 233 2/8th K.L.R. 65	

B. General
Comdg. 171st Inf. Brigade

CONFIDENTIAL.

Headquarters,

171st INFANTRY BRIGADE.

....

WAR DIARY (Special),

Feb. 20th - Feb. 29th, 1916.

....

Army Form C. 2118.

WAR DIARY
or
INTELLIGENCE SUMMARY.
(Erase heading not required.)

Instructions regarding War Diaries and Intelligence Summaries are contained in F. S. Regs., Part II. and the Staff Manual respectively. Title pages will be prepared in manuscript.

Place	Date	Hour	Summary of Events and Information	Remarks and references to Appendices
[illegible]	Feb. 1st 1916	Nil	nil	
	2"		nil	
	3"		nil	
	4"		nil	
	5"		nil	
	6"		nil	
	7"		nil	
	8"		nil	
	9"		nil	
	10"		nil	
	11"		nil	
	12"		nil	
	13"		nil	
	14"		nil	
	15"		nil	
	16"		nil	
	17"		nil	
	18"		nil	
	19"		nil	

WAR DIARY or INTELLIGENCE SUMMARY.

Army Form C. 2118.

(Erase heading not required.)

Instructions regarding War Diaries and Intelligence Summaries are contained in F.S. Regs., Part II. and the Staff Manual respectively. Title pages will be prepared in manuscript.

Place	Date	Hour	Summary of Events and Information	Remarks and references to Appendices
Canterbury	Feb 21		Nil	
"	- 22		Nil	
"	- 22		Nil	
"	- 23		Nil	
"	- 24	10.50	Orders by telephone from 57th Div. to hold 1 battalion in immediate readiness to move by road or rail as a battalion or by companies. M.G. of Brigade to be attached to this battalion	
		11 a.m	T/o O.C. 2/6" R.L.R. x 94 24.2.16 Your battalion is to be ready to move at a moment's notice AAA Remainder of Brigade to be held in readiness to move at a moment's notice AAA Load up all 1st line transport immediately Baggage and tomorrow's rations to be carried AAA Nombre 507 Coy. A.S.C. will send two G.S. wagons baggage section options to load baggage AAA Acknowledge the receipt of these orders and when battalion ready to move /"/ "Brigade"	By orderly
		11.10 a.m	I instructed by telephone by 57" Div. team wagons will not be available G.S. Limbered wagons from A.S.G of battalions not in possession of M.G. to reinforce transport of battalion held in immediate readiness.	
		11.15 a.m	T/o O.C. 2/5" R.L.R. x 2/7" 24.2.16 Your battalion is to be in readiness to move at short notice with all 1st line transport loaded including today's and tomorrow's rations AAA team [?] M.G. and M.G. ammunition in your possession with M.G. limbered wagons to report at Orderly Room 2/6" R.L.R. immediately AAA Acknowledge receipt of these orders and report transport loaded — "/" "Brigade"	By Telephone
		11.15 a.m	T/o O.C. 2/5" R.L.R. x 96 24.2.16 — (as to 2/5" — 2/7") except " Send 2 G.S. limbered wagons for M.G. to report at FOUNTAIN TAP YARD CANTERBURY for use at 2/6" R.L.R. ..."	By telephone

1577 Wt.W10791/1773 50,000 1/15 D.D.&L. A.D.S.S./Forms/C. 2118.

WAR DIARY
INTELLIGENCE SUMMARY

Army Form C. 2118.

Instructions regarding War Diaries and Intelligence Summaries are contained in F.S. Regs., Part II. and the Staff Manual respectively. Title pages will be prepared in manuscript.

(Erase heading not required.)

Place	Date	Hour	Summary of Events and Information	Remarks and references to Appendices
INTERBERG (Contd.)		12.40 p.m.	G.S. wagons B/171st batten. train found both £ to mobilize	
			1/7" K.L.R. reported ready to move (2 wagons could not be hired as other arrangements had been made, not finally reported till 4 p.m.)	
		2.15 "	— reported ready to move	
		3 "	— " " "	
		4.15 "	— " " "	
		3.30 "	Brigadier inspected transport of each battalion 1/7" were found ready. Others reported in detail.	
		4.30 "		
		4.40 "	Order from 5" Div: "S/1027 24.8.16 W/V A of the officers named in Scene S/F211 Ö.m.s will be in charge of Motor Base columns. He himself takes over his district 171st Brigade now." Replies to above Major MEYER 1/7" K.L.R. who was named accordingly.	
		7.30 p.m.	Brigade orders all battalions to remain in readiness to move at 2 hours notice. Considerable inconvenience and delay due at first to 1/6" K.L.R. not being provided with a telephone, till arrangement made to employ a private telephone near their H.Q.s, for interception communication further in a case like this, telephone is essential to ensure orders being smooth and quickly carried out. Brigade held in readiness to move at one hours notice.	
Totals: "-26"			" " " " " " " " " " " " "	
"-27"			" " " " " " " " " " " " "	
"-28"			" " " " " " " " " " " " "	
"-29"			" " " " " " " " " " " " "	

M.F.Gilbert........... Br. General,
Comg. 171st. Infantry Brigade.